THE LAST FIVE YEARS

MUSIC & LYRICS BY JASON ROBERT BROWN

For information on performance rights for *The Last Five Years* contact:
Music Theatre International **www.mtishows.com**

ISBN 978-1-4950-1587-8

HAL•LEONARD®
CORPORATION

7777 W. BLUEMOUND RD. P.O. BOX 13819 MILWAUKEE, WI 53213

Visit Hal Leonard Online at
www.halleonard.com

PROLOGUE

Music and Lyrics by
JASON ROBERT BROWN

Simply, with hesitancy (♩=120)

Segue as One

STILL HURTING

Music and Lyrics by
JASON ROBERT BROWN

Give me a day, _ Ja - mie! Bring back the lies, _ Hang them

back on the wall! _____ May-be I'd see How you could

SHIKSA GODDESS

Music and Lyrics by
JASON ROBERT BROWN

SEE I'M SMILING

Music and Lyrics by
JASON ROBERT BROWN

Steady (♩ = 80-84)

mp

I guess I can't be-lieve __ you real-ly came __

And that we're sit-ting on __ this pier. See, __ I'm

smil - ing __ That means I'm hap-py that __ you're

here.

I stole this sweat-er from _ the cos-

- tume shop _

It makes me look like Dai - sy Mae. _

See, _ we're laugh - ing _

I think we're gon-na be _ o-

kay.

I mean, we'll have to try a lit-tle hard-

-er And bend___ things to and fro___ To make___ this love as

spe-cial As it was___ five years___ a - go.___ I mean, you

made it to O - hi - o! Who knows___ where else___ we can go?___

___ I think you're real - ly gon - na like___

night, spend-ing our time, And you are gon - na choose some-one else to be ___ with ___ no, you are.

Yes, Ja-mie, that's ex - act - ly what you're do-ing: You could be here with me, Or be there with them — As

u - su - al, guess which you pick! No, Ja - mie, you do not *have* to go to a - no-ther par - ty — with the

same twen-ty jerks you al-read - y know. ___ You could stay with your wife on her fuck-ing birth - day; And you

30

could, God for-bid, e-ven see my show! __ And I know in your soul it must drive you cra - zy That you

won't get to play with your lit-tle girl - friends— No, I'm not —no, I'm *not!*— and the point is, Ja - mie, That you

can't spend a sin-gle day __ That's not __ a-bout You and you and noth-ing but you.

"Mah - ve - lous" no - vel - ist, you! Is - n't he won-der - ful? Just twen-ty-eight! The sav - ior of

I swear to God __ I'll nev - er un - der - stand __

How you can stand there, __ straight and tall, And see I'm

cry - ing __ And not do an - y - thing __ at all... __

MOVING TOO FAST

Music and Lyrics by
JASON ROBERT BROWN

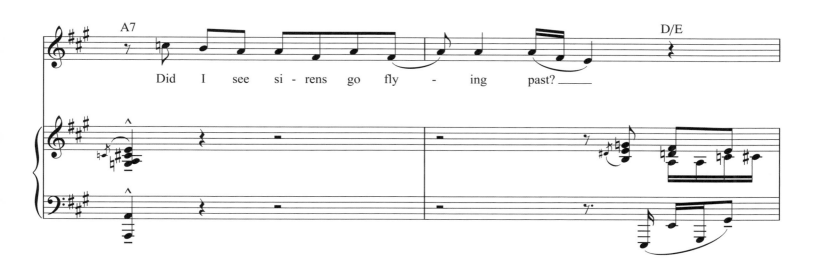

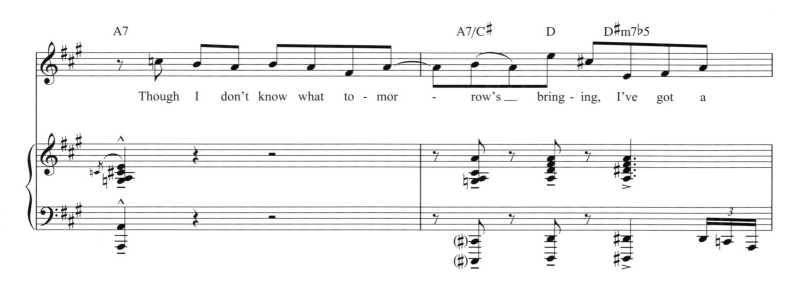

A PART OF THAT

Music and Lyrics by
JASON ROBERT BROWN

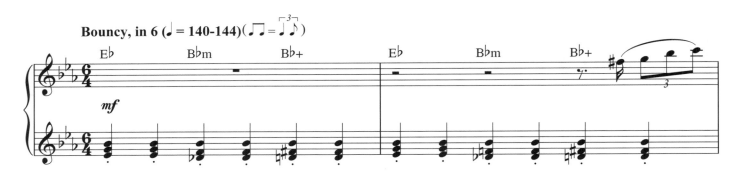

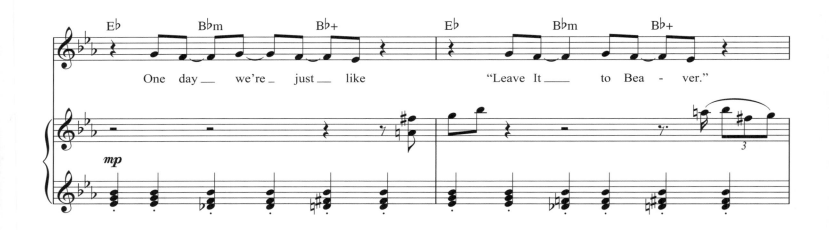

THE SCHMUEL SONG

Music and Lyrics by
JASON ROBERT BROWN

62

(♪ = ♪)

stretched his arms, and he closed his eyes, And the morn - ing sun fi - nal - ly start - ed to

rit.

mp *a tempo*

F   G/F   F   G/F

rise. _____ And the

Dm7   D/F#

dress he made on that end - less night Was a dress that would make an - y soul take flight! Not a

sempre mp

Fm6/A♭   Csus/G   C/G

swatch, not a skein had gone to waste— Ev-'ry rib-bon and but-ton i-deal - ly placed, And sewn in - to the seams Were

8va

rit. *mf*

70

A SUMMER IN OHIO

Music and Lyrics by
JASON ROBERT BROWN

Tempo di Stripper

could chew on tin foil for a spell, ___ I ___ could get a root ca - nal ___

Tempo I

___ in Hell, _ But it would-n't be as swell _ As this sum - mer is gon - na be!

'Cause the tor - ture is just ex -

qui - site ___ While I'm wait - ing for you to vis - it, ___ So

THE NEXT TEN MINUTES

Music and Lyrics by
JASON ROBERT BROWN

84

90

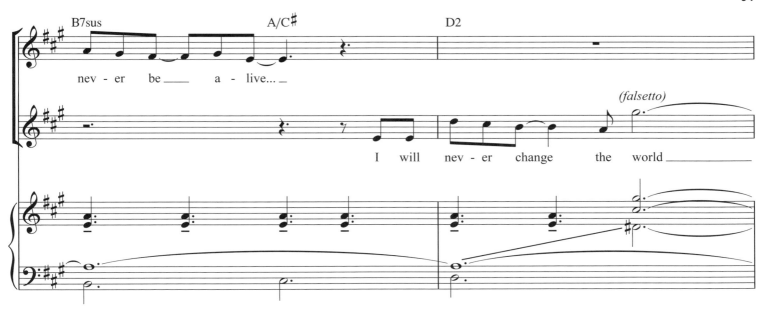

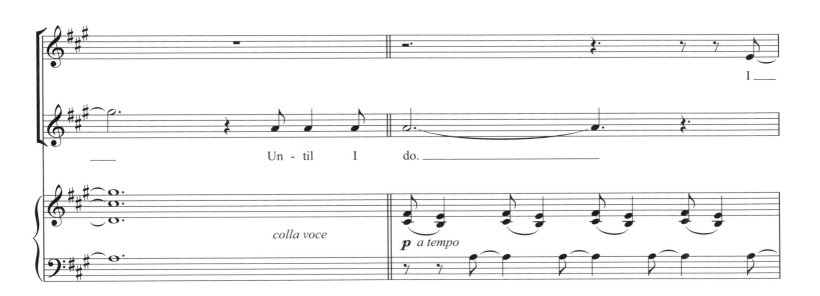

92

# pt

do. I

I

do...

do...

mf

mp

rit.

WHEN YOU COME HOME TO ME

Music and Lyrics by
JASON ROBERT BROWN

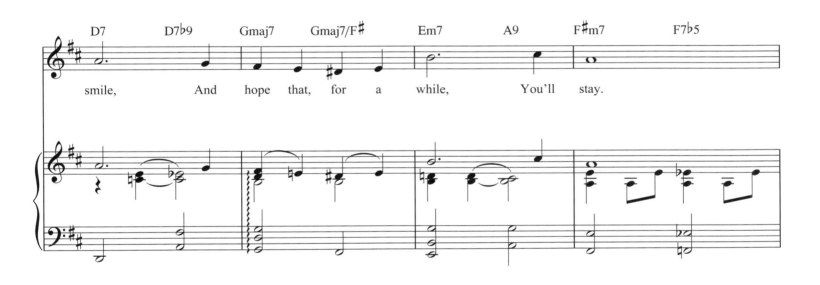

98

IF I DIDN'T BELIEVE IN YOU

Music and Lyrics by
JASON ROBERT BROWN

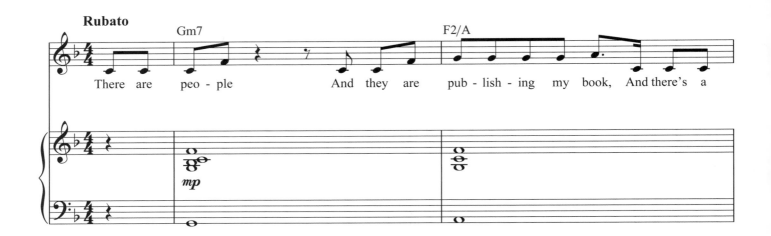

There are peo - ple And they are pub - lish - ing my book, And there's a

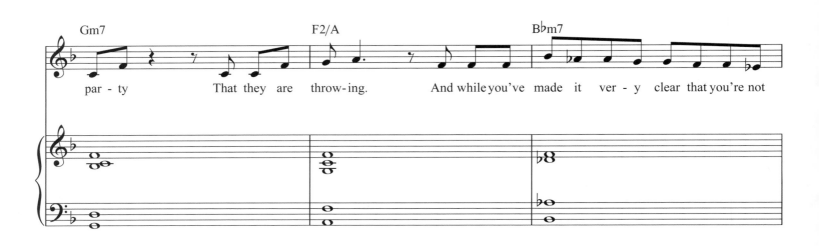

par - ty That they are throw - ing. And while you've made it ver - y clear that you're not

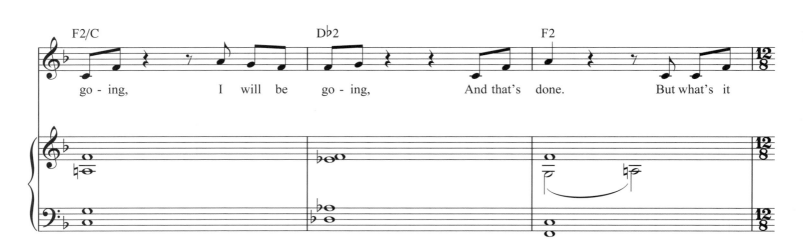

go - ing, I will be go - ing, And that's done. But what's it

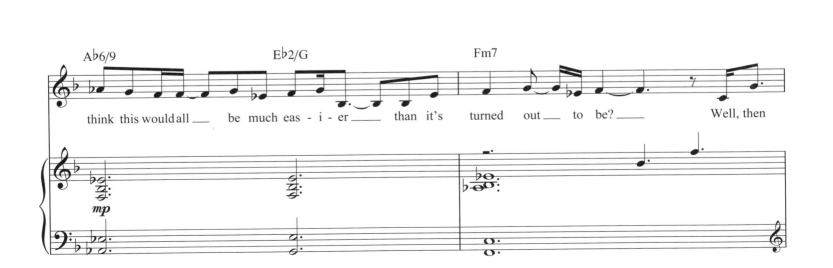

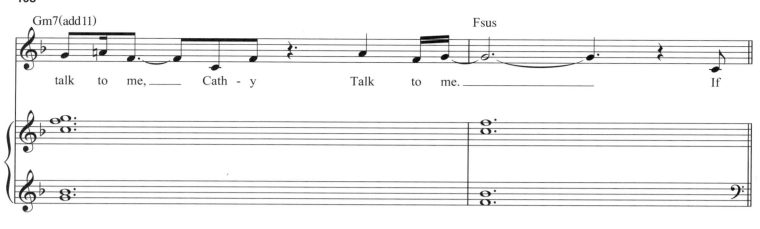

talk to me, ___ Cath-y Talk to me. _____ If

Moderato, poco rubato

I did-n't be-lieve ___ in you, ___ We'd nev-er have got-ten this far. ___ If I ___

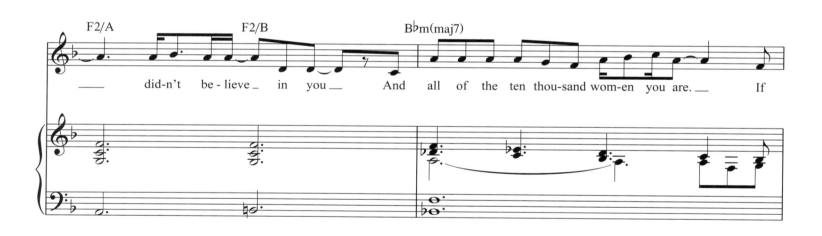

___ did-n't be-lieve ___ in you ___ And all of the ten thou-sand wom-en you are. ___ If

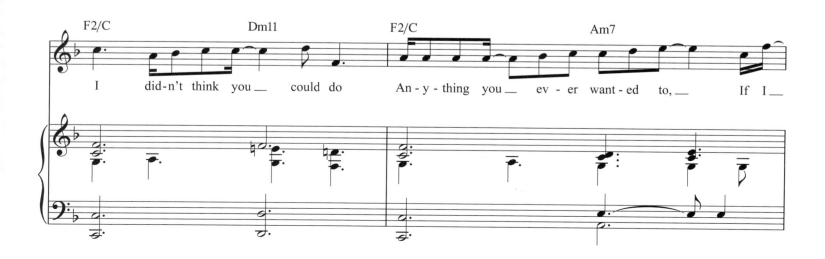

I did-n't think you ___ could do An-y-thing you ___ ev-er want-ed to, ___ If I ___

114

I CAN DO BETTER THAN THAT

Music and Lyrics by
JASON ROBERT BROWN

118

NOBODY NEEDS TO KNOW

Music and Lyrics by
JASON ROBERT BROWN

Moderato, poco rubato

Hey, kid— good morn - ing— You look like an an - gel.

I don't re - mem - ber when we fell a - sleep. ___

GOODBYE UNTIL TOMORROW

Music and Lyrics by
JASON ROBERT BROWN

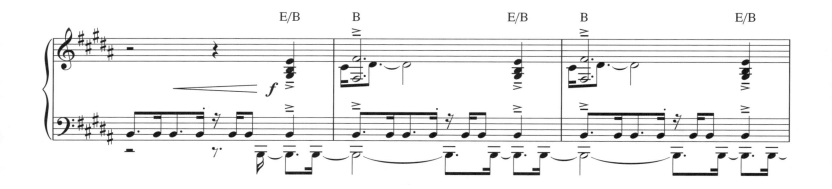

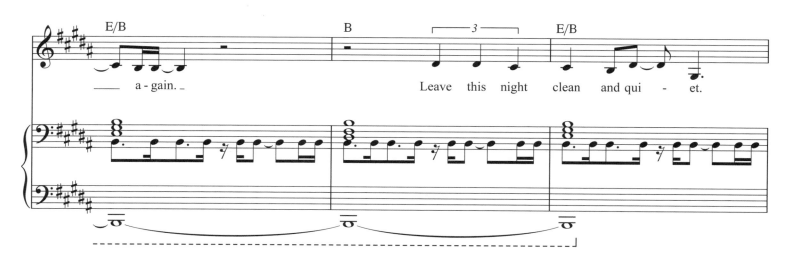